This Moment

This Moment

How to let go of what was and will be so that you can find peace and contentment in the present moment

Lidiya Kesarovska

Dedication

To all those who are trapped in their past,
carried away by their future,
limited by their expectations
and lost in their ideals.

Table of Contents

Introduction

I've always been looking for meaning in everything in life. I've also tried to see the beauty, to feel alive, find peace and contentment and eventually true happiness.

After every attempt, I was trying harder and with more pressure. As a result, I was even more disappointed when nothing changed.

When living this way, life requires too much effort and that brings stress and discomfort.

It wasn't until I calmed down, stopped looking for solutions, just started to see things as they are and appreciate them instead of trying to change them, that I finally found all the things I've been looking for. Turns out, they've all been right in front of me the whole time.

In the present moment.

It started by me being aware of it for a few seconds every now and then. But the state I was into during that time was unbelievable - I was seeing all the beauty around me and was thankful for it, I was smiling and at ease while breathing deeply and enjoying the moment. Everything was perfect just the way it was and nothing needed to be done.

I was fully aware of where and who I was in that moment. Nothing even needed to be defined, I was just experiencing and enjoying it.

No sign of thoughts about the past or worries about the future, it was just me and the present moment.

Then I realized I can live that way, not only feel like that for a brief moment, but make it a permanent state.

And although there is always room for improvement and I've got my weak moments as everyone else, I managed to achieve a lot.

I started focusing more and more on the now while eliminating distractions and trying to empty my mind by letting go of the past and future, the need to control, the desire to plan and change things.

I felt happier than ever. Grateful. At peace. And simply contented.

Everything real is in the present moment. Only here can we find happiness and harmony, feel alive and do something that will change our future. Only here can we be with the people we love, enjoy the things we like and see beautiful places.

Life is a series of such moments. And making each one matter means you're living your life to the fullest.

No ideals. No illusions. Just reality - but more perfect than you've ever imagined. That's what being mindful and living in the present means.

I've noticed that most of us don't realize how important this moment is. They take it for granted, know it's brief and think that it can't change anything. But I think it can change it all.

Try to answer the following questions:

When is the best time to live?

What should you focus on?

What is it that you can control?

What is the only thing you truly have?

What's your best present?

Where does everything happen?

Where can you find happiness?

Where can you find answers?

Where are you supposed to be?

When should you act upon your dreams?

When should you start?

These are questions you've often heard or asked. Tough ones but with simple answers. Because what they have in common is that the answer to all of them is "the present moment".

Only in it can you find what you're looking for, can you feel alive and happy, can you take action and do something about your life.

The Real Face of Suffering

What are you most afraid of?

Do you fear the future? Maybe not knowing what might happen next scares you to death.

Or is it snakes and spiders, heights, speaking in public, car accidents, the sea, or darkness that terrifies you?

What are you worried about?

Many constantly think about the possibility of losing their job, being poor, losing someone they love or being hurt.

Maybe you think you will keep failing in your love life, business, trying to get in shape or learning a new language.

Or you just compare yourself to others that seem to be living the ideal life and think that you'll never be happy.

Here's another question. What do you regret the most?

Is it that you could have become a better person, made more money by now or moved to another country?

Or do you constantly go back to the past and imagine what it could be if you did things differently?

Most people do that. And although it doesn't change anything, they keep trying to answer that "what if". And it brings them pain.

Pain that is supposed to be left far behind, kept in your memories.

But most of us seem to love going back to it over and over, to find comfort in such negative thoughts. That's how suffering comes into our lives.

It's not the car accidents, the loss of loved ones, the heartbreaks, the scary animals, the unknown, the failed business ventures or mistakes we've made that make us suffer.

None of these last for a lifetime.

Some happen in a matter of seconds, require a strong will or an action we don't really want to take. Others may take a long time to recover from.

But we keep going. We get up, try again, forget, let go and move on.

We meet new people, apply for another job, start a new relationship, try bungee jumping, learn to swim, stop driving a car or do something else after the thing we thought would ruin our life or make us unhappy has happened.

And guess what?

Nothing happens.

We keep living our life. A bit differently, of course. But the world remains the same.

So forget about poverty, possible bad situations, death and anything else that you think is the worst that can happen to you, and you might just see what actually causes suffering.

It's expecting something bad to be on the cards. Being sure that our partner will leave us. Waiting to make a mistake. Walking on the street with the chance of being hit by a car in our mind.

It's the constant looking back to the past, reliving the awful events that made you feel bad and that you keep giving power to by focusing on them.

It's not so much the job interview or the exam (and that you might fail) but the negative scenarios you play in your head before that, thinking about everything that can go wrong, fearing the moment you'll have to show up.

All that makes us suffer 24/7.

"Life is suffering. We have desires and expectations and egos, and we compare the reality we have, which is miraculous and wondrous, with this reality we desire. That somehow distances us from actually taking part fully with the reality we do have, and that creates suffering. For me, the thing that I love is that it's all about the present moment." - Alan Ball

Our minds are full of comparison, need for approval and attention, a desire to be in other places, imagining things could be better there and thus hating our reality.

We are the only ones to blame for our own suffering.

We hurt ourselves every time we think of how other people should behave according to our standards and then suffer when they appear to be individuals; every time we open a book with so many expectations about it from what we've heard and hoped it to be, and then close it in disappointment, realizing it's something totally different (maybe beautiful, inspiring and challenging, but nothing that met our expectations).

We are in pain the moment we buy something new and immediately think of a better deal we could have had. And instead of enjoying it, we regret our decision and start thinking of all the things out there we don't have.

Yes. I went so far as to say that thinking about car accidents is worse than the experience itself.

But isn't that true?

We can live with that fear for years without it ever happening. We can never walk freely near a street again, never sleep well because our kid has a license now, never become drivers ourselves and will always be stressed with public transport, can never feel the joy of having our own car or going on a road trip with friends.

All that because of a fear, a worry, an illusion we live with.

Unfortunately, we live our lives like that every day and miss out on many more things than the benefits of driving.

We can't really enjoy today because we worry about tomorrow, we can't trust a great new person because someone else hurt us before, we don't appreciate what we have because we want more, and can't thank for the life we are given because other people seem to be having a better one.

But it's time to stop that constant agony and start living, feeling, loving and experiencing.

The Origin of Suffering: What Makes Us Unhappy?

"The present moment is never intolerable. What's intolerable is what's going to happen in the next four hours. To have your body here at 8 pm and your mind at 10:30 pm, that's what causes us suffering."
Anthony de Mello

You now know what your pain really looks like. You see it from another point of view. But a deeper explanation is needed.

Obviously, our generation has a big problem - our attitude towards life, the way we see things, what we focus on and think is most important is not right.

So something needs to be done. We need to find a way to alleviate that inner pain.

But to do that, we must first get familiar with the origin of this suffering, with all the things that make us upset, disappointed, depressed, stressed, unproductive, discouraged and hopeless.

Here is a list of what makes us unhappy and what form it takes in our daily life:

1. Ideals

Most of the pain we experience, whether we realize it or not, comes from the fantasies we live in.

We create our own worlds, where there are certain rules, things to be done and said and events to happen.

Every time something doesn't go according to the plan (which, basically, includes everything because we have no control over what might happen and can't predict it), we panic.

2. Not wanting to be where you are

We create a prison, we build its solid walls slowly over the years, and can remain there for the rest of our life if we don't do anything about it.

No matter where we go, we want to be somewhere else right away. Either because we're not contented with the current place and situation and think the problem is in them, or because someone else tells us about something better.

That makes our present destination a nightmare, even if we're swimming in the ocean of a tropical island or skiing in a top winter resort.

We'll talk more about that prison later.

3. Struggle

When we feel bad, we try so hard to remove that emotion and feel better. We put effort into finding something to make us smile.

When we eventually do (or should I say 'if' we do), we struggle to make it last.

So our whole life becomes a struggle. Pushing hard, interfering in the natural flow.

But we ourselves invented this fight. It's fake. It lives only in our head and by trying too hard to succeed, find happiness, or else, we make it worse.

Here is what Leo Babauta of ZenHabits.net says about that in his book "The Effortless Life":

"We invent this struggle for many reasons: to give our lives meaning, to give ourselves a feeling of accomplishment, to dramatize our story (even if only in our own heads), or simply because this is the mode of thinking we've become used to.

Giving up the struggle isn't always easy, but it is liberating.

When you realize you don't have to struggle with everything, life becomes so much more effortless.

Take the example of struggling with your young child when she won't eat her vegetables. This struggle is unnecessary — forcing her to eat the vegetables accomplishes nothing.

The child won't like vegetables more because she's forced to eat them. Instead, set the example of eating vegetables yourself, and find ways to make eating healthy foods fun for her.

By making it fun, and letting go of the need to force her to eat veggies, you've let go of the unnecessary struggle."

4. Seeking happiness in external sources

There's a void inside most people.

It's been created by not being satisfied with who we are, not being happy with what we have, not being present and looking for something more, better, more exciting out there.

We've always been trying to fill this void with something external.

Here are some of the fake sources of happiness people turn to:

shopping - buying stuff we don't really need because it brings us short-term comfort and takes our mind away from our current problems; food - a way to feel short-term pleasure, but then we immediately feel bad about ourselves; a person - thinking someone else can make us feel good, obsessing over them, wanting to spend as much time with them as we can; drinking; gambling; etc.

It only makes the void bigger as we are okay for a while, but then feel even worse.

5. Holding onto the past

Not letting what has already happened and can't be changed go is something so bad and yet so common. Almost everyone does it to some extent.

Some people even live entirely in their past, not letting anything new happen to them, just spending their days going through stuff that happened a long time ago and has nothing to do with the present.

6. Refusing to accept

One of the reasons for not being contented is our inability to accept things as they are, together with ourselves, other people, events and every little detail of our days.

We try to change the unchangeable and control the uncontrollable, which only continues the struggle and increases our suffering.

7. Comparing

Instead of seeing your positive qualities, you focus on how much better other people look.

You see that their house is more spacious, children smarter, bank account bigger, social life better, etc.

This makes you unhappy with your life, even if you're considered successful.

8. Not knowing what's important

Often we suffer because we don't realize what's essential.

We may want to be rich, but the rich are lonely.

We see all those people on TV that have won the lottery and want to be them, but studies show that they are even more miserable after having won the big check.

They don't really know what to do with all that money, take poor decisions on how to spend it, change themselves and their friends don't see them in the same way.

9. Being a victim

If you're constantly asking the universe "Why me?", then you probably think life is unfair, others are so much happier and you'll never be, or just take things too personally and make a big drama out of small things.

10. Worrying about what might happen

Living in the future is another reason we struggle so much. That's why there's a whole chapter for it later in the book.

11. Goals

Living without goals may seem a bit too much for some of you, but what I mean with that item of the list is that goals are another version of living in the future, focusing on a result that's not part of our present moment, wanting something else and expecting it to become a reality.

Here's how Leo summarizes it:

"These days, however, I live without goals, for the most part. It's liberating, and contrary to what you might have been taught, it doesn't mean that you stop achieving things.

It means that you stop letting yourself be limited by goals.

Sometimes you achieve a goal and then you feel amazing. But most of the time you don't achieve them and you blame it on yourself.

Here's the secret: the problem isn't you, it's the system! The goals system is a set up for failure.

Even when you do things exactly right, it's not ideal because goals limit your possibilities. When you don't feel like doing something you have to force yourself to do it. Your path is chosen, so you don't have room to explore new territory. You have to follow the plan, even when you're passionate about something else."

12. Plans

The same goes for plans. Here's Leo's take on that:

"Living without plans might seem foolish or unrealistic to most people. That's fine. But if you want to be realistic, you should understand that the plans you make are pure illusions of control.

Many days, other things come up and the illusion of control is easily shattered. But some days we get lucky and our plans actually happen as we had hoped.

The more we embrace this chaos, the more we embrace the brilliant possibilities that might emerge.

The more we try to control our day and actions with plans, the more we limit ourselves."

13. Expectations

This refers to not being happy with the person you've become and the things you do because you have too big expectations of who you can be.

Or when you want your partner or someone else to do something for you, love you in a certain way, be nicer, ask you out, etc. You expect so many things from them, often unrealistic. You wait for them to do exactly what you imagine. But people have their own vision of the same situation and it rarely meets yours.

You even ask life for more than it can give you and become unhappy when you understand it has its limits too.

14. Wanting to change

Kids want to be grown ups, adults want to be young and careless again.

Single people desperately want a relationship, but those who are in one still complain almost all the time and wish for freedom.

The poor want money, the rich want more of it.

This means that changing your situation doesn't prevent you from suffering, doesn't make your desires go away. You need to change something on the inside instead.

But what can we do about all these 14 things that constantly ruin our attempts to be happy and peaceful?

A Simple Solution

"Having spent the better part of my life trying either to relive the past or experience the future before it arrives, I have come to believe that in between these two extremes is peace." - Unknown

Simple, yet mind-blowing, the answer can be found in something small that's right in front of your eyes all the time.

I'm talking about the present moment. About this beautiful brief part of your life.

Here is how it happens to be the secret to freeing yourself from all the negative things mentioned in the previous chapter:

Ideals - once you are fully present, you don't need these fantasies anymore. You just live in this reality and know it's the best it can be in this moment;

Not wanting to be where you are - you're more than happy to be here, right now. You don't need anything else and make the most of the situation by experiencing it;

Struggle - you're relaxed, all the stress and the desire to try hard to be happy are gone, and you simply find contentment in the present moment;

Seeking happiness in external sources - there's no need to turn to anything that's outside of your mind and body. You yourself are enough and by being given this moment, you can live in the best way possible;

Holding onto the past - mindfulness helps you understand that the past is gone, can't be changed and all the lessons are already learnt. Now you need to move on, freer than ever, and experience new things;

Refusing to accept - once you feel powerful, peaceful and contented at the same time, you will be more than okay with things as they are;

Comparing - now you know you can't compare this moment to any other, because once you experience it with your whole being, you know it's unique and won't happen again. Also, you can't compare it to any previous one. Just as you can't compare yourself or your life to those of others;

Not knowing what's important - feeling alive and focused will help you realize that all the happiness, love and peace you've been looking for are in this moment. It's the most important thing right now, together with the people around you and the place you are at;

Being a victim - no person that has ever felt the benefits of being present can consider themselves a victim or unhappy in any way. You see all the beauty around you, you're inspired, you feel deep appreciation and gratitude;

Worrying about what might happen - it's another thing that doesn't concern you right now because it's about a place different from this one. Thinking about it can only ruin your now;

Goals - no need for them, everything's perfect already;

Plans - when you feel one with the whole world, absolutely present, confident, worthy, thankful and full of joy, you can't really make any plans because that will mean you have to change something;

Expectations - you let go of the ideals of how others should behave and how you expect things to turn out and simply enjoy what is, the way it is;

Wanting to change - you've accepted things, appreciate them, feel free and contented. There's no need to do anything to change it.

Now let's dive into the details of how the magic happens - how to let go of the past and future, stop wanting things to be different, accept, enjoy and find peace.

But first, let's see how that mental prison looks like again and how to break free from it.

The Prison You Live In and How to Get Out of It

"We can easily manage if we will only take, each day, the burden appointed to it. But the load will be too heavy for us if we carry yesterday's burden over again today, and then add the burden of the morrow before we are required to bear it." - John Newton

Every place you don't want to be at feels like a prison. We have so many desires, expectations and go back to the past and think about the future so often, that I can safely say that we live in a prison all the time.

Every time you wish you were somewhere else right now is another solid wall you build and thus make this imaginary building even stronger.

Every time you wait for the weekend to come because you hate your job (which means you live 2 days out of 7), every time you can't wait for your summer holiday to come, whenever you go back to your memories and wish things could be as easy as they were when you were a child, or else, you tell yourself that you're not satisfied with where you are now.

You may not realize it but that's how you ruin your happiness and peace and have started living in a never-ending cycle of regrets, memories, imaginary situations, plans and expectations.

Every single thought that is connected to a state you were at and wish you could bring back or a guess of how things may turn out tomorrow, is another time you harm yourself. You destroy your joy and contentment which can be found only in the present moment.

That's also how stress comes into our lives. More often than not, we welcome it with open arms.

It has become a way to deal with things - we prefer to worry about what might happen or feel bad about things we can't change from the past and that's how we avoid facing problems, or a simple thing like trying to focus on this moment because it causes us discomfort.

That's the prison we live in.

While it can be pretty hard for prisoners to escape the real one, the walls of yours are just imaginary and can be gone just the way they were created - by using your mind, by changing the way you look at things.

The key word here is acceptance.

Your life looks like a prison because you focus on the things you wish you had and thus don't appreciate what you already have.

So why don't you try to see the abundance in your life? Because if you haven't noticed, you've got many things to thank for. Just look around.

Then simply accept them. Accept yourself for the person you are, for all the mistakes you made and also for the transformation you're about to experience in the future. Love your future version right now.

Accept others for the way they behave and think, don't expect them to be anyone else but themselves. That will save you the trouble of being disappointed once they don't react the way you imagined them to.

Then try to be grateful no matter what happens. Understand that nature knows what it's doing and things turn out just the way they should. Not always the way you want them to, though. That's why if you learn to go with the flow and just be okay with every turn of events, you'll be a happy person in no time and that prison will be gone.

After doing that you'll start to like the place you're at in each moment. You will appreciate it, find its good sides and know that you should be there at that exact time. The future is uncertain and later you may end up being somewhere else, but then you'll also find peace there as it will be just the place you should be at - just a different one.

That's the simple way to reach peace of mind.

Not to escape the prison or destroy it. But to just get out of it without hurting anyone and stay right where you are with a smile on your face.

You're not a prisoner anymore. You can now live freely and happily in the present moment and enjoy all its benefits.

3 places

"The meeting of two eternities, the past and future....is precisely the present moment."

Henry David Thoreau

In life we've got many choices. One of them is to decide where to spend this moment. There are 3 options:

The past

You can think about what happened yesterday, analyze it, wish it was different, regret your mistakes, be upset about the things you couldn't do or the opportunities you missed.

You can go back a few weeks ago or even years and do the same. There are always things to regret, things that could have been better, words that shouldn't have been said, memories to remember, hard moments to relive and people's reactions to try to understand.

The future

You can also think about the stuff you have to do later. Maybe you won't have enough time so let's be disappointed in yourself now.

What about tomorrow? So many bad things can happen, your plans may not work out, you may not feel good or do anything interesting.

Many people spend their days worrying about what tomorrow will bring. They try to prepare for it, to keep things under control, they expect a certain series of events. But the result is different and that makes them feel useless and hopeless.

The present

Then there's the third place you can choose to be at - right here, right now.

But you'll need to forget about yesterday and tomorrow, accept them as they are - learn from the past and be at peace with it, let it go; then let things be and look forward to what the future has in store, but don't try to change it.

So which one looks better?

I guess your answer is the third option. I think so too.

I need to ask you this then (myself included): Why do you keep dwelling on what has already happened and worry about what might happen one day?

That's one of the most common and yet ridiculous and self-destructive human habits. We do it all the time.

But there are ways to avoid it, get over it, eliminate it. It starts by learning and understanding why we do it, how it harms us, what causes it and - of course - what to do to start living in the present and feel its benefits.

Here is something I know for sure that I keep repeating to myself as part of my meditation in the morning:

"Yesterday is gone. I've done my best and there's nothing else I can do about it. So I let it go.

Tomorrow is uncertain, I have no idea what's going to happen and it shouldn't bother me now because it's going to be the best thing that can happen. But until then, I don't need to worry about that.

And here I am now, having the whole day in front of me. It is the only thing that matters. Today I can do the best I can, work on my goals, smile as much as possible, be grateful, appreciate everything and be mindful.

It all begins with this moment. It's the only thing I can control, so I choose to grab it and make the most of it."

Now let's learn how to let go of what was and what will be so that we can embrace this beautiful moment and make peace with it.

After all, life is a series of such moments. Making each one matter means living a life of fulfillment, happiness, gratitude and purpose.

How overthinking causes suffering and what to do to stop it

An old friend of mine was working as a waitress in a bar some time ago. One of the regular guests asked her a question one day after his usual few drinks. He wanted her to tell him the year of an event that was important to the history of our country.

It's considered that everyone should know these dates, but if we have to be realistic, the only time we actually talk about them and learn them is at school. After that most people never need to mention them again simply because they don't encounter a situation in which they have to think about it.

But being asked that by an older person and not knowing the answer always makes us feel a bit stupid and even ashamed.

That's how my friend felt. Not that there was anything she could do about it in that moment, but she was upset the whole evening.

She thought the man chose to ask her from all people in the bar because she looked stupid and just wanted to check if he was right about that.

She remembered comments her parents and teachers made over the years when she didn't have good results on tests.

She felt bad because deep inside she knew she hadn't done her best most of the time. She started thinking that maybe she wasn't doing it then as well. She looked around the bar and asked herself where her life was heading.

A few days after that the same man came in smiling and went directly to her. He said he finally learnt the date of the historical event and from now he was going to know it too.

She then understood that he himself never knew it and expected her to have the right answer.

So the whole thing was actually a compliment

That's a simple situation from our daily life that's not very significant. But it's a great example of how ridiculous overthinking is and how harmful it may be.

***

17

Imagine yourself walking down the street. Someone passes by and looks at you for a few seconds.

Most people immediately start thinking that there's something wrong with them: maybe they have something on their face, walk in a funny way, aren't dressed properly, aren't good-looking, etc.

They can go on like that for hours or even days. Then they become even less confident and want to avoid looking other people in the eyes for some time.

The truth is that the person who stared at you was probably lost in their head, thought you look like someone they know, found you interesting, liked you, or else. The possibilities are countless and what you think is almost never right.

How overthinking causes suffering?

Overthinking makes us see things that aren't really there. We get lost in thoughts and from a single daily situation we've interpreted wrong, we can come up with the conclusion that our life sucks, that we'll never find love or that our dreams will never come true.

We think about the things we wish we had, regret what we've missed out on and couldn't do, think about how things would turn out if we acted differently.

We lose ourselves in a reality so different from the present moment.

We stay there and become depressed and disappointed, lose hope and can't find peace. That's how suffering comes and it never goes away until we let go and focus on the now.

How many times have you caught yourself obsessing over a future event and playing different scenarios in your head? Or analyzing a painful memory over and over again and feeling worse after each time?

Too many, I'd say.

That behavior, that mental habit of giving birth to thoughts and ideas that are not real or have already happened and nothing can be done, is destructive.

We don't even take action as a result of that thinking. We just ruin our present by not experiencing it, by focusing on a past event or a future imaginary situation.

It's a harmful behavior. Basically the mind goes over situations (big or insignificant) and starts to wonder why they happened, what the person did wrong, whether it could have been better and how, what it means, whether it will have consequences in the future.

The answers, however, are never good or real.

Why is thinking bad most of the times?

All that refers not only to negative thinking but to overthinking in general.

Because we're almost never right in our assumptions. Our lack of self-confidence and determination, and living with the fantasies of how things should turn out, is what makes thinking a burden.

Here is how Eckhart Tolle describes it in his great book "The Power of Now":

"Not to be able to stop thinking is a dreadful affliction, but we don't realize this because almost everybody is suffering from it, so it is considered normal. This incessant mental noise prevents you from finding that realm of inner stillness that is inseparable from Being. It also creates a false mind-made self that casts a shadow of fear and suffering.

Thinking has become a disease. Disease happens when things get out of balance.

For example, there is nothing wrong with cells dividing and multiplying in the body, but when this process continues in disregard of the total organism, cells proliferate and we have disease.

Note: The mind is a superb instrument if used rightly. Used wrongly, however, it becomes very destructive. To put it more accurately, it is not so much that you use your mind wrongly - you usually don't use it at all. It uses you. This is the disease. You believe that you are your mind. This is the delusion. The instrument has taken you over.

Let me ask you this: can you be free of your mind whenever you want to? Have you found the "off" button?

-You mean stop thinking altogether? No, I can't, except maybe for a moment or two.

Then the mind is using you. You are unconsciously identified with it, so you don't even know that you are its slave. It's almost as if you were possessed without knowing it, and so you take the possessing entity to be yourself. The beginning of freedom is the realization that you are not the possessing entity - the thinker. Knowing this enables you to observe the entity. The moment you start watching the thinker, a higher level of consciousness becomes activated. You then begin to realize that there is a vast realm of intelligence beyond thought, that thought is only a tiny aspect of that intelligence. You also realize that all the things that truly matter - beauty, love, creativity, joy, inner peace - arise from beyond the mind. You begin to awaken."

The reason why overthinking harms us is clear: because it's not connected to the present moment, which means it's not real and evokes negative emotions in us that shouldn't be there.

Only when you think about where you are now, focus on your current activity, see the things around you and thank for them, speak with the people around you about positive things, and think about how beautiful and perfect all this is, are you thinking right.

Thinking too much also makes us lose direction in life and then take the wrong one. It destroys the vision we have in our mind of our purpose, goals and dreams and we don't see clearly anymore. From then on, we're stuck.

Often people's reaction is to blame others instead of taking responsibility for creating their own prison and choosing to live in it. But that's just another way to escape reality, their decision and the results of it.

We're so used to thinking stuff like that that we do it most of the day or night. Some can't even sleep. That's how stress comes into our lives and later forms diseases.

Fortunately, there is a solution - there are things we can do to stop overthinking and live with a free and peaceful mind.

How to stop overthinking

"The best gift we can have is living in the present moment and really enjoying it for what it is; and, not being in our heads and getting sidetracked." - Amy Smart

1. It all begins with acknowledgment.

Realize you're doing this and accept it.

Things are this way and you're behaving like that. Okay. But you can change it.

2. Forgive yourself for falling into this trap and be compassionate.

Many others are there, actually most people. It doesn't mean there's something wrong with you. You just didn't see it when it all started.

3. Act and start now.

Action is what changes our reality. If we get up and do something about our problem, we will have progress.

Here is what author Bob Miglani says about that in an article on Huffington Post:

"One tip that I've learned that did more than detox my mind from over thinking is to turn my often worrisome thoughts about the future into effort and work. Taking action, doing something, working on your craft does wonders for your soul.

Each time I would start getting worried about the future, I would make a proactive choice to physically get up from the

place I was sitting and walk to the computer to start writing or working on my book. Sometimes I would go outside to work on planting the tomatoes in my vegetable garden. If I was at work during the day, I started writing ideas on how to improve my work or work on something really interesting. Whatever the work or project we choose — make sure it is a difficult one because that's when we start to get flow or momentum. That's the place where so much of our success happens."

4. Small steps.

Start, but start small. That's a golden rule and it always precedes change.

Overthinking is a habit and you'll have to approach it like you would any other. Small changes over time will lead to a huge transformation.

Start by writing down your thoughts when you catch yourself thinking too much. Or set a goal to notice doing it and stop immediately. Replace thoughts like that with positive ones.

5. Learn to empty your mind every now and then so it can rest.

Meditation is a great choice. I myself practice it when I can: sit down in a place with no distractions, focus on your breathing and empty your mind.

Don't put a lot of effort, don't try too hard. Just let go of all thoughts because you don't need them. Breathe deeply and feel clarity and freedom.

Do it for a few minutes every day for a start. Then you'll be able to keep it for longer and soon you'll see the benefits this little habit has.

You'll see that you feel contentment, joy and peace when your mind is still and no thoughts about the past or future are in it.

6. Be okay with things.

Look around. See the world as it is, the people in your life and yourself for who you are. Accept it. Realize everything is just as it should be.

Then you'll feel relieved because you won't need to change anything, you won't need to control it or worry about what would happen.

You'll just experience, mindfully.

7. Forget perfection.

Our ideals, illusions and the desire for perfection are slowly killing us.

You won't feel happy and contented in the present moment until you let go of them. Acceptance is the answer.

No need for things to be perfect because they already are.

8. Appreciate the abundance in your life.

Become aware of the present reality with all its beauty, opportunities, great people, chances to take, places to see, things to do. It's brilliant!

There's no reason to think about it. Just live it. It's your now and it's the only thing you have.

Thinking about what was or what will be makes it insignificant and you miss this fleeting moment.

But if you feel the abundance around you and thank for it, you'll see how much you have.

You'll understand it's more than enough, and then you won't need to change it. So there won't be any reason to think that much.

9. Distract your mind.

The goal is to stop thinking about a certain event, obsessing over a person, planning too much or imagining different scenarios. Distracting yourself is a simple but useful step to take.

Find a hobby, go out, meet friends, watch a movie, work out, etc.

But distraction works for some time - only until it heals a part of your pain, bad memories, anxiety or else that causes thinking too much.

Stressing continues as we keep going back to that vicious circle even when a single thought about what we're fearing, planning or doubting pops up.

Then there's one thing left to be done.

It's the most powerful, beneficial and magical process and once we learn how to do it, we become free, in harmony and find bliss by being able to live in the now.

Letting go of the past

Letting go means accepting life as it is, not judging, being okay with things and letting events come freely and naturally. When we go with the flow and move on in life by just experiencing the present moment, we learn to let go of what was and what will be.

The truth is that it doesn't matter what has happened before or what may or may not happen in the future. The only thing that should matter to all of us is to be aware of this moment. Because it's all we have, all we possess and can control, all we need and all we can enjoy and feel.

Everything else must be eliminated for it is not essential.

In this chapter of the book and the next one, I'll take you through the process of letting go of the past and future by explaining why we don't need to think or worry about them, how they harm us, how to free our minds from them and start living in the now.

This will result in happiness, peace and contentment and we'll feel more alive than ever before.

How dwelling on the past hurts us?

"You can clutch the past so tightly to your chest that it leaves your arms too full to embrace the present."
Jan Glidewell

Almost every single person has spent a great deal of their life thinking about past events, regretting the things they did or didn't do, imagining what it could be if they did things differently, or just experiencing moments again in their head so that they can understand what went wrong.

That's just another way to escape reality, to avoid facing current problems and things we need to think about. But doing it by going back in time, where nothing can be changed, and just causing more pain to ourselves is illogical.

You can't have peace now if you still think about yesterday. You carry with you all the burden, bad feelings, emotional conversations, things that hurt you, fears and doubts, and you bring them into your present and future. But they don't have any place there. They must be left in the past.

We use the past as an excuse. One of the many we live with.

Most of the time people find it easier to hold on to what happened instead of moving on. So they escape there, relive events all over again because it feels familiar and thus create another prison where they spend a significant part of their life.

That's sad because we're missing out on the beauty of this present. On all the opportunities, people, places and activities around us. Instead of smiling, laughing and living life to the fullest, we prefer to be alone with our thoughts of the past and rethink what's already history.

This is so harmful. I'd go even further and say that even learning from the past may be bad for us if we're used to such a behavior.

The moment we remember it, we experience it again. Here's an example:

It's not a rare thing these days for a person to start thinking about someone who's hurt them. We may have had our heart broken in a past relationship with someone we cared about. Instead of letting go by accepting it, we decide to spend our days trying to find an explanation that will make us feel relieved.

THIS MOMENT

We remember in detail the moment the person told us they didn't want us anymore. We feel that pain as if it's happening now. We're bringing these feelings back to our present. And although nothing can be done now, we suffer.

It's a self-destructive behavior because we're the ones causing it.

The other person has nothing to do with it, actually. They have probably been honest with us, and no one said that we're the problem. Maybe they just needed some time alone to figure things out. Or had other problems they needed to focus on.

But we decide to think of the most negative reasons for the breakup. We think we're not good enough, are absolutely sure we did something wrong, and assume we won't be in a relationship anytime soon, or ever again.

Then we don't see any meaning in doing anything else - like working out to get fit or working harder to get promoted - because we'll end up alone anyways.

Our mind can play such tricky games and is quite good at it.

The only way we can stop it, though, and go back to living freely and happily is to learn to let go.

I said learn to do it, not just to let go once because it's a continuous behavior. It's not just important to accept your past now and move on. You need to be ready to let go of it the moment something has already happened.

Take the good from the situation, smile about it, be grateful for the lesson, breathe deeply and move on. That's how we should all live.

Another reason why we ruin our present and future by thinking about the past is that we focus on the bad parts of it.

We keep remembering and reliving our failures and bad relationships and it's no wonder that the next one will be the same and we will fail again.

Because of what has happened, you see yourself as a failure even in your present. You're not confident, you don't believe you can do better or change, you deny your chances and good qualities and don't love yourself.

So if you don't want to repeat the past, if you want to move on, to feel freedom and be able to have new amazing experiences, you need to simply let go.

Here is how:

Be grateful instead - thank for everything that has happened.

Take the lesson - realize you're stronger, more experienced and powerful now and take these qualities to your future.

Focus on the now - it's where past and future don't matter, it's where you feel, enjoy and live.

Eliminate - you don't need to have people in your life that remind you too much of things you want to forget, or objects that are painful memories, or watch movies or listen to songs that evoke bad feelings. Get rid of all that.

Forgive - forgive everyone for the way they treated you, and forgive yourself for the times you didn't do the right thing or missed out on an opportunity.

Realize that the problem itself is not a problem, but thinking about it is - you did the best you could and now you can do even better. So no regrets.

Change - you can't change by going back to what was, but you can do it by taking action now and doing something about your life in the present moment.

Know that holding onto stuff and people is actually harder than letting go - understand that and allow freedom and peace to come naturally to you by emptying your mind of past mistakes. The moment you think about them again is the moment you give them power. But if you focus on the now, everything will be just perfect.

Living in the future

"You can always cope with the present moment, but you cannot cope with something that is only a mind projection - you cannot cope with the future." - Eckhart Tolle

Many of us want to know what their future looks like.

But you don't need to go to a fortuneteller to know the answer. I can tell you, right now. And I'm going to be 100% right.

Your future is uncertain.

In the face of uncertainty, the best thing you can do is stop worrying about what's going to happen and pay attention to your present.

Stop trying to guess what tomorrow will bring, doing everything possible to get prepared, worrying, fearing, obsessing and stressing over it.

Let go of the need to control and change. It's what prevents you from living your life right here and right now.

We all want to be sure that our future is secure, but security is an illusion.

Again, it's our idea of how events should turn out, how people will react and how our life will be. We expect that so much that in the end we're disappointed to such an extent that we totally ruin our present by being upset.

So here are the 2 main things that make us live in the future and what to do about them:

1. Expectations (ideals)

2. A desire to control and change things (perfectionism - you don't accept anything the way it is and try hard to make it match your version of how life must be).

We expect so much from ourselves, other people and life and it's always different from reality. That's how disappointment comes.

Let's take relationships, for example.

We expect our partner to behave in a certain way, to think the way we do, to say and do stuff we imagine them to. But that's just how we want things to be, and it's rarely how they turn out.

We open ourselves to disappointment the moment we start expecting something.

We create these scenarios in our mind of what's going to happen next and they become our second reality. But it never meets what's really going on in life and we end up being miserable. We lose hope and don't trust people anymore. This is so sad.

My advice is this: **stop expecting, start accepting.**

Only when you stop trying to change people, will you be able to see who they really are and enjoy their company.

Only when you stop interfering, will you be able to accept whatever happens and make the best of it.

Acceptance is what we need more of. It's the ability to be okay with things and just be sure that they turn out in the best way possible.

Not only do we expect, but we do it too much. We often forget that people and life itself have limits too.

Understanding the nature of life means accepting it for what it is in each moment. It may be better or worse and there's only one thing you can do about it - be present.

Only then will you be living in the best way possible.

Be kind to this moment. It's the thing in front of you, it's happening right now - be part of it. Live it and experience it. Together with the people next to you, or the place you're at, or the sounds and smells around. Care for all that as it's all you got.

As long as you're able to be aware of the beauties of the present moment, you'll live happily.

So ditch expectations. Let go of all those ideals that are ruining your now. Perfectionism is slowly but steadily destroying our ability to live life to the fullest and be mindful. It makes us live in an imaginary world where everything happens according to our expectations and we get disappointed every single day.

You don't have to live like that. Freedom and contentment are right in front of you - in this moment.

But don't expect it to be great, to feel in a certain way, to last long, to be better than a previous one. Try to just let it be. Then you'll see what it's capable of and will be amazed by its power.

If we learn to do that, living in the future becomes pointless. Worrying about all these little daily things, making plans and setting goals, being afraid that something bad may happen and wanting people to behave in a certain way - all this just doesn't have any place in our life anymore.

THIS MOMENT

We've seen what the present can offer us now and past and future are just what was and what might be - but they don't exist or matter at all in the now. So we don't need to think about them.

That frees us and lets us be who we really are and go with the flow. Slowly, naturally, beautifully. That's how things are in this moment and it's all yours.

Another thing I wanted to mention in this section is waiting. Please don't do it anymore.

Don't wait for the next moment to come to see what will happen. Does it really matter if it only makes you eager and miss out on this one? No, of course.

It's in the future, it's uncertain. Making assumptions doesn't do any good to anyone.

Instead, let go of that and be here. Look around and have a taste of the present. It's the best thing that can happen to you right now and no other moment after it can be any better - it will just be different.

Waiting is a waste of time. You may spend your whole day waiting for the moment you'll go to bed because you're tired, but then before you go to sleep you'll be looking forward to tomorrow because you have something to do that can't wait. Then for the weekend, next holiday, another goal of yours, summer, etc.

This way life becomes a waiting room.

But it's not. You make it so. You can get out of there right away by letting go of what was and will be and staying present - focusing on the things happening here and now.

Why do you need to wait for something when there won't be any better time to do it than now?

Live the life you live now, love the person you love now, say what you want to say now, do what you want to do now, later may never come.

This is the only way to make every second count and thus have a happy, fulfilling life.

The barriers to peace of mind

"There is one thing we can do, and the happiest people are those who can do it to the limit of their ability. We can be completely present. We can be all here. We can give all our attention to the opportunity before us."
Mark Van Doren

Mastering living in the present moment and feeling all its benefits can only be achieved if we learn how to have peace of mind.

That means leaving all distractions, worries, fears and non-essential things behind and letting in the power of the now, the importance of the current situation and the peace and joy that go with it.

But so few people have reached that state. There are barriers that stand in the way of being happy and appreciating this moment without thinking about anything else.

Below I'm going to talk about the main things that prevent us from being peaceful and what to do about them.

1. Desires

We've got countless desires. At least a dozen of them ruin the present moment every time we try to focus, just breathe and stop thinking and enjoy life.

I want you to realize something now. Just think about it.

Having many desires right now and giving these thoughts power by focusing on them means we're not quite satisfied with where we are.

For example, wanting to buy something means our life is not good enough and we assume it may get better if we possess that.

The truth is that we're seeking temporary happiness again and trying to find it in outer sources like material stuff, when actually it's right here, in front of us.

Being present means concentrating only on what's around us right now, wherever we are. It means that the only thing we should care about is the current situation, because nothing else really matters but the thing that's happening now.

The same goes for the things we have. They are here right now. The best we can do is appreciate and enjoy them and not think about what else we can buy.

Wanting something means you're not happy with the way things are and are looking for a way to change that. But by doing so you interfere with the natural flow of events and thus ruin this moment.

All this shows you're dissatisfied with your current life. Without contentment, though, there's no mindfulness and presence.

So when you desire, you're not really living your life. You're just moving from one outer source of potential happiness to another. It's time to realize that you don't need to change anything in your environment or life to find it. You just need to find peace in this moment.

That happens by letting go.

You can start appreciating things as they are now and feeling the abundance in your life. When you let go of all desires and unnecessary needs, this moment will unfold its beauty to you.

Then you'll have joy and freedom.

2. Thinking

There was already a whole chapter about that as there are a few important points to be made, so I'll be brief here.

Thinking too much is a great barrier on our way to living consciously. It makes us create unreal situations, guess, make predictions and so on, without knowing the facts. That makes it pointless and it only harms our peaceful existence.

Sometimes, unfortunately, even thinking itself is bad. People have gone so far that they need to analyze every little detail of their daily life. To label it, give it different meanings, compare it to other things they know or have heard of.

That literally destroys the beauty of everything. So again, let go, empty your mind and be present.

3. Comparing

Here's something we've all witnessed:

A young boy receives a present. He loves it. He truly enjoys it for a while until he understands a few things.

First, he notices that a friend of his has a better version of this item. That makes him feel bad. Then a few more boys show up having the same, worse or better. It means his present is not unique anymore as everyone seems to be having it.

Then he remembers other stuff he's always wanted to have and now that seems nothing compared to them. He realizes that shops are full of other toys like that. In his imagination, he starts creating even more incredible images of it.

Now his life is worse than before having received the present.

That's what comparing does to us. We do it at every stage of our life no matter how grown up we are.

We constantly compare our lives to those of others and somehow they always seem better.

The truth is that there's always going to be someone richer, better looking, with a bigger house, more successful, with more friends, who is more outgoing, whose kids are behaving better, whose life seems more interesting, who is more charming, etc.

We can list a hundred comparisons right in this moment if we start thinking about it.

But if we are objective, it's all pointless. Because no two people are alike in any way, and no two lives can be compared.

You can't even compare two people of the same age who've been raised together. Each one is an individual, has different opinions, goals, dreams and personality. Wants different stuff from life and has different ideas on how to get it. Has been through completely different situations that have made them the way they are.

So let go of comparison. It's meaningless, it's only an illusion and most often makes you feel worse about yourself.

The same goes for the present moment.

Most people can't experience it because they compare it to a previous one or one from the future.

But it's unique. It's never happened before and will never be repeated. So only if you enjoy it now and be here mindfully, will you be able to make the best of it.

Stop trying to find similarities by thinking about a moment you've already experienced, or trying to guess whether the next one is going to be better. Whatever you think, you'll be wrong.

Simply let go, and let this moment be what it is.

4. Measuring

Another funny thing we do all the time is measuring.

When we do something, we think about its time length - we wonder how long it will take us, whether we'll make it on time, what we're going to do next, etc.

Without realizing, we're lost in thoughts again and taken far away from the here and now.

But when you stop measuring time , you let go of it and start enjoying what is.

***

Just do it. Let go of the past and future because they don't really matter now. The only thing you should be measuring is the peace in your mind and joy in your heart.

Now you know the 4 main things that don't let you live your life to the fullest in the present moment. The next step is to do something about that.

But don't look at them the way you look at hardships and problems, don't treat them like enemies.

They are barriers just because you've made them so. In reality, they are just random thoughts that can easily be avoided, just some time ago you've decided to hold onto them. You can easily let them go.

Show understanding and compassion, just as you would to another human being. That's how peace comes. Not by resisting but by accepting.

So first accept these 4 things that you dedicate so much time to. They are part of you right now. But in the next moment they can be let free just by letting go of them.

How to be present

"Realize deeply that the present moment is all you ever have. Make the Now the primary focus of your life."
Eckhart Tolle

You already know that the most important thing is to let go of the past and future so that what is left will be the present moment.

But there are also other ways to be present. Learning to do all of the following is what will give you the peace, freedom and contentment you're looking for.

Single-task

In order to be able to really focus on what you're doing in this moment - whether it's working, studying, communicating, reading, watching a movie, walking, driving, eating, meditating, or else - you'll need to do one thing at a time.

Do you ever wonder why some people look so busy on the streets?

It's not because they are actually doing important stuff all the time.

More often it's because they have many tasks on their list (most of which don't really need to be done), have no time for all of them and are always in a hurry, and do at least two things at a time (like drinking coffee, talking on the phone, reading something and thinking about the meeting they have in an hour) which results in bad performance.

They are not efficient or concentrated and waste too much time, energy and effort on leading such a lifestyle.

But a conscious person, one that has decided to work on their habits, change the way they look at things and simplify their life, would choose to do just one thing at a time but do it with all their attention.

Single-tasking lets you get stuff done, be present and have great results. It allows you to become one with your current activity, without comparing it to what you've done before or worrying that you won't have enough time to finish it. Distractions like that are unnecessary.

Observe

Another way to be mindful is to notice every detail that's part of this moment.

Look around. If you're meditating, for instance, feel your breath, pay attention to the thoughts that come into your mind, hear the noises around you.

When you're out, see the people passing by, walk mindfully and focus on every step you take.

You can do this with every activity in your day. Drinking coffee, eating, talking to a friend, brushing your teeth, etc. It's an easy and great way to become aware of what's in front of you and to experience it fully.

Go slowly

What's with all the rush? I find that so pointless.

Slow down. You've got time.

Start doing the things you do in a new way - by noticing them, appreciating them, doing what needs to be done without any fast movements, not jumping from one task to another but slowly finishing one and then moving on.

Eating more slowly will let you enjoy the food and really taste it; walking more slowly will help you breathe the fresh air, notice the smells and noises around you.

Meditation

To meditate is to simply sit down and be present. Nothing more.

But almost no one can do it from scratch. That's because we're so used to having countless thoughts in our head every second and think about everything else but this moment.

So in order to meditate, which will then bring you peace and happiness, you'll need to let go of all that planning, judgment, comparison, memories, goals, visions and ideals.

You'll need to simplify things as much as you can.

Then breathe deeply and empty your mind. That's when you'll feel freer than ever.

Eliminate

Get rid of everything that's not important in the present moment, ignore all distractions, forget the past, don't think about the future.

Nothing else exists but you, what's happening right now and this moment. So be here, live it, and make the most of it.

Mindfulness

"Act in the moment, live in the present, slowly slowly don't allow the past to interfere, and you will be surprised that life is such an eternal wonder, such a mysterious phenomenon and such a great gift that one simply feels constantly in gratitude." - Osho

Although I talk about it throughout the whole book, I'll dedicate a short section only to mindfulness. I do that because it's one of the most important things when speaking about the present moment and finding peace and contentment, and people still have trouble defining it.

Basically, mindfulness means living this moment - enjoying it instead of being in a rush to get rid of it because you find it unpleasant or just because you're looking forward to the next one.

It means being awake - experiencing everything around you, and alert - noticing even the small things, feeling them not just thinking about them.

It's our ability to be sensitive, to go deep into this moment and find its meaning, see its beauty, use all our senses to be aware.

This can be practiced and our awareness can increase over time.

That can happen by reminding ourselves every now and then of what's happening right now and that it's the only important thing and nothing else actually deserves our attention in this moment.

You see without judging and comparing, accept things as they are - that's what being mindful means.

When you're mindful, you never forget what's important.

You also have better relationships because you listen and understand others, communication is clear and simple as you don't let other thoughts pop up in your head and stay concentrated on what the other person is saying or feeling.

Awareness is a bliss. It's the thing we all need more of in order to start living life to the fullest and embrace its beauty.

Right now most people lack this quality. They live unconsciously. They do things on autopilot, have many thoughts about the past and future, are always busy with tasks but never focus on the current activity, don't actively listen when they communicate, most of the time don't know what's going on and are like in a dream.

But they wake up, they start to really see the world. Suddenly, all the things they considered problems, fears and worries become so insignificant compared to the gratitude, positivity and focus they have now.

This emotional freedom is just a step away. Empower yourself in daily life by becoming aware, by living slowly - one moment at a time, and knowing that it will pass, it's disappearing and won't be repeated. That will make you appreciate it, be kind to it, not fight it but actually experience it with your whole being.

What Can You Find in The Present Moment

"There is surely nothing other than the single purpose of the present moment. A man's whole life is a succession of moment after moment. If one fully understands the present moment, there will be nothing else to do, and nothing else to pursue. Live being true to the single purpose of the moment."

Yamamoto Tsunetomo

The benefits of living in the now are mentioned in different ways in every chapter of this book, but here are all the things you'll bring into your life once you start being present:

1. Peace

We have everything these days. All the tools, belongings, ways to connect in a matter of seconds, sources of information, all kinds of food and cosmetics, places to go, ways to get there, and so much more.

But one thing we're missing is peace of mind.

It appears to be the most important thing we need in order to be able to handle the difficulties of life and still be able to enjoy it.

The best and probably the only real way to find it is by learning to be mindful and live here and now.

Anxiety, stress, depression, negative thoughts, constant worries, fears, regrets - these are the things someone that's not at peace has to deal with throughout the day. That's not easy.

Instead, why don't you let go of past events, future plans and worries, and start seeing only what's happening right now?

That little change in your attitude towards life will transform your whole world.

2. Joy

Pure contentment can be found only in the present.

Once you make it a habit of yours to be present, focus on the now and be one with the activity you're doing, you'll become happy.

Happiness is not in past mistakes or future uncertainties. It's here - in this place, with these people, being this version of yourself, doing whatever you're doing. It's the best that can happen to you in this moment.

3. Appreciation

Learning to do all this will also teach you to be thankful for what you have.

Because you'll be constantly focused on the things around you, you'll notice the abundance you live in.

That makes you grateful and you appreciate everything. As a result, you enjoy it even more.

4. Productivity

We're obsessed with being productive and completing as many tasks as we can.

But we never really manage to do that without feeling exhausted and stressed afterwards. Our performance is rarely good.

But if you think about it, the only time you can actually get something done is now, and the only place is here.

So that makes it even more important to know how to be present. Because if you're working on your tasks in the present, you're more likely to get things done and be satisfied with the result.

5. Stillness

The busy modern life doesn't let us relax properly and some people never have any quiet time for themselves. This moment gives you the chance to be still, at peace, at ease and just enjoy the silence.

It doesn't really matter whether you're outside and there's a lot of noise and distractions around you. If you focus on being present, you'll empty your mind of all that and will manage to have some pleasant time without being interrupted (not only by people and notifications, but also by your own thoughts).

6. Freedom

I don't think that a person who thinks about the past and future too much can be called free. They basically live in the prison of their memories and illusions.

You can't really feel what it's like to live in the now if you don't free yourself from that burden and start being mindful.

Freedom is another thing you can find in the present. It means letting things be the way they are and enjoying them to the fullest.

Not being under the control of your fears and worries and not being limited by your plans and goals. You should try it because freedom feels pretty great.

Aren't these things wonderful and wouldn't you love having them in your life? Especially when it's so easy and simple - by truly experiencing each moment of your life and enjoying it.

Inspiration: What Others Say About The Present Moment

1. Let life happen to you. Believe me: life is in the right, always. - Rainer Maria Rilke

2. Life is all memory, except for the one present moment that goes by you so quickly you hardly catch it going. - Tennessee Williams

3. The secret of health for both mind and body is not to mourn for the past, worry about the future, or anticipate troubles, but to live in the present moment wisely and earnestly. - Buddha

4. The present moment is changing so fast that we often do not notice its existence at all. Every moment of mind is like a series of pictures passing through a projector. Some of the pictures come from sense impressions. Others come from memories of past experiences or from fantasies of the future. - Henepola Gunaratana

5. Forever is composed of nows. - Emily Dickinson

6. You must live in the present, launch yourself on every wave, find your eternity in each moment. Fools stand on their island of opportunities and look toward another land. There is no other land; there is no other life but this. - Henry David Thoreau

7. The only way to survive eternity is to be able to appreciate each moment. - Lauren Kate, Fallen

8. You never know what the future holds. Something that seems bad today could end up to be something good tomorrow. You might meet the love of your life at the second job you had to take to make extra money. The Universe works in mysterious ways. Your only job is to keep showing up and staying open to hope. - Denise Ryan

9. It is through gratitude for the present moment that the spiritual dimension of life opens up. - Eckhart Tolle

10. We should not fret for what is past, nor should we be anxious about the future; men of discernment deal only with the present moment. - Chanakya

11. The power for creating a better future is contained in the present moment: You create a good future by creating a good present. - Eckhart Tolle

12. If you abandon the present moment, you cannot live the moments of your daily life deeply. - Nhat Hanh

13. While you are meditating, if your mind wanders, gently bring it back to the present moment. - Sharon Salzberg

14.Anything you're trying to will is focused on the future; it's always associated with some sort of anxiety that makes the present moment somewhat uncomfortable. - Martha Beck

15. Most people treat the present moment as if it were an obstacle that they need to overcome. Since the present moment is life itself, it is an insane way to live. - Eckhart Tolle

16. All I have is all I need and all I need is all I have in this moment. - Byron Katie

17. All the Buddhas of all the ages have been telling you a very simple fact: Be – don't try to become. Within these two words, be and becoming, your whole life is contained. Being is enlightenment, becoming is ignorance. - Osho

18. Wherever you are, be there totally. If you find your here and now intolerable and it makes you unhappy, you have three options: remove yourself from the situation, change it, or accept it totally. - Eckhart Tolle

19. One of the most tragic things I know about human nature is that all of us tend to put off living. We are all dreaming of some magical rose garden over the horizon – instead of enjoying the roses that are blooming outside our windows today. - Dale Carnegie

20. Pile up too many tomorrows and you'll find that you've collected nothing but a bunch of empty yesterdays. - The Music Man

21. Look at everything always as though you were seeing it either for the first or last time: Thus is your time on earth filled with glory. - Betty Smith, A Tree Grows in Brooklyn

22. When you take your attention into the present moment, a certain alertness arises. You become more conscious of what's around you, but also, strangely, a sense of presence that is both within and without. - Eckhart Tolle

23. The present moment, if you think about it, is the only time there is. No matter what time it is, it is always now. - Marianne Williamson

24. The answer is, who you are cannot be defined through thinking or mental labels or definitions, because it's beyond that. It is the very sense of being, or presence, that is there when you become conscious of the present moment. In

essence, you and what we call the present moment are, at the deepest level, one. - Eckhart Tolle

25. Life gives you plenty of time to do whatever you want to do if you stay in the present moment. - Deepak Chopra

26. If my happiness at this moment consists largely in reviewing happy memories and expectations, I am but dimly aware of this present. I shall still be dimly aware of the present when the good things that I have been expecting come to pass. For I shall have formed a habit of looking behind and ahead, making it difficult for me to attend to the here and now. If, then, my awareness of the past and future makes me less aware of the present, I must begin to wonder whether I am actually living in the real world. - Alan Watts

And here is what Leo Babauta says in the "Effortless Life":

"We try to hold onto the illusion of control, but what if we instead embraced the chaos? What if we leave ourselves open to the changing, unfolding moment, and the possibilities we could never plan for?

It's beautiful.

Try it. Throw out your plans for the next hour. See what happens, moment to moment. Think about what excites you, what's in line with your values. Be intentional about this.

And as you start doing things that excite you, things that are in line with your value... see what new things emerge. Talk with people with no fixed intentions, and see what ideas arise from those interactions. See what new opportunities evolve as you interact with people, with ideas, with your own thoughts.

It sounds nebulous, but in fact it's as concrete as anything else. As I've shown, when we make plans, we think we're setting things in concrete, but life is always fluid—we just try to make ourselves believe that it's solidly concrete.

When we acknowledge the fluidity of our lives, we learn to use that fluidity to our advantage. We flow. We are open to changing currents. We see things with open eyes, instead of trying to make the world adjust to our plans and goals.

I don't have all the answers, and, in fact, I'd be a hypocrite if I claimed to be able to predict what will happen when I live like this . . . or if anyone else lives like this.

I don't know what will happen. Think of the limitless possibilities of that simple statement."

Further reading:

The Power of Now: A guide to spiritual enlightenment, Eckhart Tolle

The Book of Awakening: Having the life you want by being present to the life you have, Marc Nepo

Focus, Leo Babauta

The Effortless Life, Leo Babauta

A Little Book of Contentment , Leo Babauta

The One Skill, Leo Babauta

The Tao of Pooh, Benjamin Hoff

Net, blog

StevePavlina.com, blog

BuddhistSocietyWA, YouTube channel

Cover Image

Photo credit: flickr.com/photos/charlietakesphotos/

Changes were made.

About the author

Lidiya Kesarovska is a blogger, course creator, business mentor and the founder of Let's Reach Success where she helps people build an abundant, value-driven business so they can live a fearless life and serve their purpose.

She's been named one of the top 10 course creators and experts to watch in 2021 by Yahoo! Finance, been featured on TIME magazine, Thrive Global, Disrupt Magazine, and more.

Lidiya is also the host of the Free and Fearless podcast, has been in the personal development and online business industry for over 7 years now, and has welcomed thousands of students into her business programs.

With the content on her blog and the courses she creates, she shares the steps to ditch your limiting beliefs, unleash your potential, start that side hustle, grow it strategically, and use that income to live your best life & be unapologetically confident!

She's devoted most of her life to personal development and reclaiming her freedom by building a digital business. Now, she's obsessed with helping you do the same!

Resources & Contact

Head to letsreachsuccess.com to find countless resources on personal development and business.

Email Lidiya at lidiya@letsreachsuccess.com to ask anything you feel like or just say Hi.

Read her whole story at letsreachsuccess.com/about

Go to letsreachsuccess.com/courses for the programs and trainings she offers in case you want to take this work to the next level.

She's also the host of the Free and Fearless Podcast if you prefer audio content. You can find it on any major podcasting platform by searching for the show there. Or just go to letsreachsuccess.com/fearless to check out the latest episodes and subscribe.

Instagram: instagram.com/letsreachsuccess

Twitter: twitter.com/lidiyasblog

LinkedIn: linkedin.com/in/lidiya1/

Pinterest: pinterest.com/letsreachsuccess/